CULTURAL
IMPERIALISM

I0162807

Robert Cecil

1971

MONOGRAPH SERIES NO. 6

The Institute for Cultural Research

About the Author

ROBERT CECIL, CMG, MA WAS Chairman of
the Graduate School of Contemporary
European Studies, University of Reading
(1976-8), and Chairman of the Institute
for Cultural Research, for which he edited
an anthology, *The King's Son* (Octagon
Press, 1980). His other published works
include *Life in Edwardian England*
(1969), *The Myth of the Master Race:
Rosenberg and Nazi Ideology* (1972),
Hitler's Decision to Invade Russia
(1975), *A Divided Life: a biography of
Donald Maclean* (1988), *and The Masks
of Death: Changing Attitudes in the
Nineteenth Century (1991).*

This monograph is the text of a lecture delivered under the aegis of the Institute for Cultural Research.

Cultural Imperialism

I OUGHT to begin with some definition of how I am using these two words: cultural imperialism. I want to use the word imperialism in the sense of the impact of a race, people, or nation, which in ordinary politico-economic terms is strong, upon another race, nation or people which in politico-economic terms is relatively weaker. The impact of the strong on the weak is usually treated in the history books in terms either of conflicts, colonial wars, wars of independence and so on, or else in terms of political organisation – the Indian empire, the American colonies, Commonwealth, French Union and so on. The way I want to deal with it is in terms of the confrontation of two cultures, because we have today the idea, and it's a comparatively modern idea, that the culture of the country, or the continent in the case of Europe, which is stronger in terms of technology, weaponry and political organisation, must also have a culture superior to that of the country, or group of countries – often we call them developing countries – which do not possess the same technological and other advantages. This is, in fact, a comparatively modern idea; the Romans, for example, although in political and economic terms, in organisation and so on, much stronger than the Greeks, were quite prepared to admit that Greek culture was superior to their own. Similarly the barbarians, as they were called, who destroyed the Roman empire, were quite willing to admit that they had much to learn culturally from the Romans. So this is a comparatively modern development, of which I shall say more in a minute.

Culture, of course, I am using not in the narrow sense, the sense in which it has been said that culture is found in museums and galleries on wet Sunday afternoons, but in the broad sense of culture as a manifestation of the psychic life of a people. In particular, I am going to talk about it in terms of language, education, metaphysics and religion. There is also a very useful definition of culture, a very succinct definition, in a book by the American anthropologist Edward T. Hall, which some of you may have read. He quite simply says that culture is communication, meaning that it is through the cultural life of peoples that they can communicate with one other; but also, as I am going to illustrate tonight, it can be something that tends rather to divide them.

Obviously I cannot talk about all the different imperialisms, all of which have somewhat different connotations, Spanish, Portuguese, Dutch, Russian and so forth. I am going to concentrate on Anglo-Saxon Imperialism, British and American that is, and to some extent also on French, for the reason chiefly that the British and the French expanded into the same continents at about the same historical periods. Because first contacts between cultures can be so important, I am going to begin with the impact of the British and French on the original inhabitants of

North America, the American Indians, and then to some extent also on the peoples of the Indian sub-continent. Then I shall take a few side-glances at Africa and, coming on to the present day, I want to examine the question whether cultural imperialism is really dead, or whether it has merely taken new forms.

Now to begin with something of an historical perspective, how did the Europeans acquire this rather arrogant attitude towards non-European cultures? It is an attitude that was very well expressed in a phrase I found in a contemporary French writer the other day, who said, 'There is something sad, pathetic even, in the efforts of certain intellectuals to prove that the culture of their country of origin is the equal of European culture.' It is an extraordinarily arrogant remark when you come to think about it. I have already said that in the classical period of history the assumption was not made that, because you could outfight other peoples, therefore you also had a culture which was superior to theirs. The Renaissance in Europe, which opened a great many new horizons, was largely based on the rediscovery of Greco-Roman civilisation, much of which had been preserved in the medieval civilisation of Islam. Then in the eighteenth century, the period of what is often called 'the enlightenment', when the intolerance and exclusive attitude of the churches, which had contributed so much to separating European from Islamic culture, had dwindled, the idea grew stronger that reason was common to all mankind, in all parts of the world and in all ages of history, even pre-Christian periods;

hence one should have at best an interest in, and at worst a tolerance for, the exotic non-European cultures. So there was in the eighteenth century a keen interest both in non-Christian antiquity and also in exotic non-European cultures, including relatively primitive ones (or ones which the Europeans regarded as primitive).

This was perhaps most clearly expressed in the thinking of the French '*philosophes*'. For Rousseau's followers, for example, the North American Indians represented a form of society relatively uncorrupted by what they regarded as tyrannical forms of government and society in 18th century Europe. Another French writer, La Bruyère, said, 'Reason belongs to all climates.' They concluded from this that every European should take an intelligent interest in the civilisations and cultures of remote parts of the world. For these French 'philosophes', the North American Indians seemed to supply an example of the relatively happy, enlightened 'savage', as they called him, from whose form of existence something could be learned. From this came the stereotype of the 'noble red-man', something which degenerated later in American minds into the Hiawatha type and later still into the 'Cowboys and Indians' syndrome. The French took up this line of thought because they came to North America not as settlers so much as hunters and travellers and they found the Indian useful. They took an interest not only in the way the Indians made their living, but also in what they thought and how they lived.

The British, by contrast, had come to Plymouth Rock and Jamestown as settlers. They wanted land and they wanted labour, so they decided that the Indians were nomads and they took their land. As the Indians still refused to work for them, they imported negroes as slaves. The British, of course, didn't invent negro slavery on the American continent; it had been introduced in the 16th century by the Spaniards in the West Indies. I do not want to spend very much time on slavery because it represents the least fruitful contact between two cultures – the maximum of exploitation by the more powerful and the minimum of effort to bring about any kind of human contact.

Why, then, if the 18th century was relatively enlightened, did it allow slavery to continue and indeed to develop? I think there are two main reasons for this. First, in the eyes of the Europeans, white and black were at the extreme ends of the spectrum; particularly the negroes from Africa seemed to the Europeans quite extraordinarily different from themselves – almost a difference of kind rather than of degree. But secondly, and I fear more importantly, the negro slaves were absolutely essential to the economies both of the sugar islands in the West Indies and of the cotton and tobacco states in the south of what shortly became the United States of America. The maintenance of the cultural standards and the standard of living of the whites depended on denying any cultural standards to the blacks and debasing their standard of living. Yet in the long run the slaves in the North American continent fared better than the red Indians because, as the doctrine of what the Americans called the 'manifest destiny' evolved

– the destiny to overspread the whole North American continent – the Red Indians were either exterminated or driven into reservations. Parallel to this development there was created the new stereotype of the Red Indian, not now the noble Hiawatha type, but the image of either a bloodthirsty warrior – this is of course the 'Cowboys and Indians' syndrome which persists on television to this day – or else the lazy, drunken good-for-nothing. But the Red Indian was drunk because the white men sold him cheap liquor and he was idle because they had taken his land. Once the strong had created a stereotype of the weak to suit his economic convenience, it is not very difficult to bring reality into line.

In fact, if there had existed any real contact between the two cultures, the white men could have learnt much from the red men. The white men might have learnt, for example, some respect for nature and the need to conserve natural resources. The Pueblo Indians cultivated what is now Oklahoma with wooden ploughs and with restraint, where later the white farmers turned it into a dust bowl. The red men fished the Great Lakes and got their living by it, where the white men have so poisoned the lakes with industrial effluent that no fish can now live in them. Secondly, the whites might have learnt from the red men some respect for ancestors. Instead the Americans acquired a great contempt for the past and evolved the worship of youth. This was, of course, partly promoted by the massive scale of immigration and the fact that the children, brought up in American schools speaking fluent English, acquired in this way a contempt for their own parents, who still spoke broken English and clung to the out-of-date way of life of the European countries from which they had come. Thirdly, the whites might have learnt from the red men the virtues of open-handedness instead of the get-rich-quick of the affluent society. An American anthropologist has written of the American Indians: 'In the main a man was respected because he gave, not because he possessed.' Of course there was an interchange and the red men acquired from the white the horse, which was very valuable to them; but they also acquired measles, firearms and liquor, and not many of the benefits of the consumer society.

I should like to turn now to Asia. The British had gone to North America to settle, but they went to India to trade and for this reason at first they made no attempt to disturb Indian society or to impose European religion and culture on the indigenous people. The first Governor-General of India, Warren Hastings, founded a college for Arabic and Persian studies in Madras and his successor Lord Cornwallis (the same one who had had an unfortunate experience at Yorktown) founded a college of Sanskrit studies at Benares. The 18th century, as I suggested earlier, believed that there was something of interest in alien cultures. Sir William Chambers erected a pagoda in Kew Gardens, which you can see to this day. George the Fourth erected at Brighton the Pavilion, which has been described as 'pseudo- Hindu without and pseudo-Chinese within.' When in the last of the year of the 18th century Napoleon went to Egypt, he took with him architects and draughtsmen to study the monuments there and he circulated all over Europe transcriptions of the Rosetta stone in the hope, which was realised, that the wise men of Europe would eventually be able to decipher it. Napoleon said, though he did not always live up to it, that 'True conquests, the only ones which leave no regrets behind, are conquests over ignorance.' After this promising start in India, what went wrong? First, I think, as British rule expanded all over India, problems of administration grew. Lord Cornwallis believed every native of Hindustan was corrupt and concluded that it was necessary to Anglicise the administration. In 1806 the East India College, now known as Haileybury College, was created to produce the Indian Civil Service, as it came to be called. Secondly, after 1813 Christian missionaries were admitted to India and they tried not only to convert the heathen, but also to change their way of life, some aspects of which they very much disapproved. Into India, where religion permeated all aspects of Indian life, they imported the curiously European idea that religion was some special compartment of the mind and emotions, separated from the daily life of political expediency and economic self interest. They imported also the dualistic idea, foreign to the Indians, of an antagonism between soul and body and mind and matter. Thirdly, in the 1820's, the Utilitarians, followers of Jeremy Bentham and the principle of the greatest happiness of the greatest number, imported into India the idea that prosperity and, in their view, therefore happiness, consisted in economic progress and improved education and material conditions for all, a belief that on the whole exists to this day. Finally, under the influence both of the Evangelicals and the Utilitarians, although they were not in agreement with one another, the British in India developed a strong sense of mission. They believed that they had the duty to interfere in the way of life and culture of the peoples subjected to their rule and to convert them to the European way of life, which they believed to be in every way superior. The Indian Civil Service was forbidden to trade; they were to concentrate on administration and they began to proselytise; this was the beginning of the phase to which we usually give the designation 'the White Man's Burden.'

The watershed was the Governor-Generalship of Lord William Bentinck (1828–35) with at his elbow for part of the time Lord Macaulay, an evangelical, and in the India Office James Mill, sometimes described as the Saint of Rationalism, a utilitarian, who at this time, although he had never visited India, was writing his great History of India. Bentinck believed that the key to civilising the Indians lay in what he called, 'The British language, the key to all improvements'. Persian, which had been the language of the higher courts of Law, was replaced by English as the official tongue and there began a period when, although the Indian Civil Service learnt Indian languages, they gradually ceased to have any interest in Indian thought and Indian culture. 'General education,' said Bentinck, 'is my panacea for the regeneration of India.' Instead of doing as his predecessors had done and subsidising Persian and Sanskrit studies, he decided that all funds available for education should in future be spent on English language and Western science, because this would make the Indians rich and therefore happy. But cultural contacts, unfortunately, were not altogether happy. To take one example from the Law, Macaulay himself observed and commented on the unfamiliarity of the Indians with the English Common Law. This is what he wrote in his essay on Warren Hastings: 'No man knew what was next to be expected from this strange tribunal. It consisted of judges not one of whom was familiar with the usages of the millions over whom they claimed boundless authority. Its records were kept in unknown characters, sentences were pronounced in unknown sounds. It had already collected around itself an army of the worst part of the native population, informers and false witnesses and common barrators and agents of chicane and above all a banditi of bailiff's followers.'

If you turn to another field of abortive interchange, the British succeeded in teaching the Indians to have wants, to have needs, although in Indian philosophy nothing was less desirable than desire. But there was no reverse flow, as far as the British were concerned, and this can be illustrated from the life of John Stuart Mill, the son of the James Mill, whom I have already mentioned. Like his father, John Stuart Mill felt contempt for Indian philosophy and religion. He was convinced in early life by the utilitarian belief that it was possible to achieve the greatest happiness of the greatest number by educational and economic reform; this was the secret. Then in 1826 he suffered a period of terrible depression, which he wrote about as follows in his autobiography: 'In this frame of mind it occurred to me to put the question directly to myself. Suppose that all your objects in life were realised, that all the changes and institutions and opinions that you were looking forward to could be completely effected at this very instant, would this be a great joy and happiness to you? And an irrepressible self- consciousness distinctly answered "No"! At this my heart sank within me: the whole foundation on which my life was constructed fell down. All my happiness was to have been found in the continual pursuit of this end. The end had ceased to charm, and how could there ever again be an interest in the means? I seemed to have nothing left to live for.' Yet even this harrowing experience does not seem to have led

Mill to investigate the possibility that another people in another and more distant clime, pursuing a very different way of life from that of the Europeans, might also have thought about such problems, have experienced such depressions and produced an analysis of them which might at least have been worth investigating. Mill's contempt for the wisdom of the East persisted.

During the 19th century the penetration of imperialism was sharpened and made more acute by two fatal theories. First, Darwinism took hold – not in the form in which Charles Darwin propounded it, but in the form in which some of his followers tried to adapt it to human societies. This was the theory that the fittest societies to survive would be the strongest societies, and strongest, of course, in the 19th century meant having the maxim gun and repeating rifle; those who had these ruled because it was their right to rule. Secondly, there emerged the theory of racialism, first propounded by the French diplomatist, Count Gobineau, and then developed by a renegade Englishman, Houston Stewart Chamberlain, who married a daughter of Richard Wagner and went to live in Germany. The theories of these racialists, overlaid with Social Darwinism, led to the idea that purity of race was something in itself desirable – based on a very dubious analogy with the with the breeding of greyhounds and racehorses – and that if you could breed a pure race it would be the strongest and therefore the fittest to survive. So there was gradually drawn up in their minds a kind of league table of races, with Teutons and Anglo-Saxons at the top and Jews and Negroes at the bottom.

These theories were unfortunately in vogue just at the time when the British and the French were spreading out in Africa and when British rule in India was being reinforced after the Mutiny. What I am saying may sound a little exaggerated, so I am going to quote from Macaulay an extract which illustrates this 'league table' concept very well. Macaulay, who was writing about a Bengali of whom he disapproved called Nuncomar, says this, 'What the Italian is to the Englishmen, what the Hindu is to the Italian, what the Bengali is to other Hindus, that Nuncomar was to other Bengalis ... The physical organisation of the Bengali is feeble even to effeminacy. He lives in a constant vapour bath. His pursuits are sedentary, his limbs delicate, his movements languid ... His mind bears a singular analogy to his body. It is weak, even to helplessness, for purposes of manly resistance; but its suppleness and its tact move the children of sterner climates to admiration, not unmixed with contempt ... Large promises, smooth excuses, elaborate tissues of circumstantial falsehood, chicanery, perjury, forgery are the weapons, offensive and defensive, of the people of the Lower Ganges.' It has curious overtones of a headmaster of a British public school in the tradition of Arnold writing a report on one of his less athletic boys.

I do not want to belittle the genuine British achievement in India in terms of harbours, roads, bridges and hospitals, which still remain; but there was no fruitful interchange of ideas and no mutual respect. The British never really grasped that their success in India had been due not to racial superiority but to their technological advancement and to the different organisation of Indian society, which was not divided into nation states, each keen to defend its frontiers, but horizontally according to caste and vertically according to religion. This distinction was not grasped. Again I would quote the contemporary opinion of John Lawrence of the Punjab, who said in 1858, 'We have not been elected or placed in power by the people, but we are here through our moral superiority, by the force of circumstances, by the will of providence. This alone constitutes our charter to govern India.' Another Victorian statesman, Sir Charles Dilke, said, after travelling widely throughout the Empire, 'The idea which in all the length of my travels has been at once my fellow and my guide – the key to unlock the hidden things of strange new lands – is the conception of the grandeur of our race, already girdling the earth, which it is destined perhaps to overspread.' It never seems to have occurred to him that this attitude of superiority blinded him, in fact, to any understanding of 'the hidden things of strange new lands.'

This was the period of the White Man's Burden. In America it took the form of manifest destiny, which I have already mentioned, and it was also strong in the minds of the French spreading out at this time over Africa. The French were faced with a particular problem, because they were not only the heirs to the capitalist system and therefore wanted colonies for economic reasons, but they were also the heirs to the French Revolution and they had to believe in equality, liberty and fraternity. Therefore the black men had to be brothers, but the French were Big Brothers, and this fostered the idea inherent in the French civilising mission, according to which the greatest service that a French man could render to a black man was to make him as much like a French man as possible. Two different kinds of alien culture developed in Africa, so that on one s1de of the Niger River little anglophone children would be reciting multiplication tables, while on the other bank of the river francophone children would be mouthing Racine.

Having dealt, albeit rather sketchily, with the historical part, let us come up to the present day. Has all this changed? Have we really abandoned all the trappings of imperialism, or are we just pursuing the same objectives in a different and perhaps rather more subtle way? The former colonial powers today claim to be reformed characters, and it is true, of course, that instead of extracting profits from their colonies they have set them free and supplied them with aid and technical assistance. But is this in fact setting them free? Open attempts to dominate these countries had begun to meet with increasing resistance. But if one creates appetites, which only western technology can satisfy, does one not tie what one calls the developing countries to one just as effectively as by having an Empire? Let me try and illustrate this. If the sole aim of aid and technical assistance were to raise the standard of living in these countries, why could this not be done by contributing money to the United Nations or other multilateral agencies to distribute this aid? In fact, of course, both Britain and France give ten times as much aid bilaterally, that is in agreements country by country, as they do in the form of contributions to the United Nations. 25% of British aid and nearly 50% of French aid is in any case in the form of loans tied to purchases from the mother country giving the aid. Over 75% of the aid of both countries goes to developing countries which were formerly their colonies and indeed 60% of all French aid, which is on a substantial scale, goes to French-speaking countries which together have only 1% of the population of all the third world – the developing world – added together.

What are the instruments which are used? The chief of them is language, because if you oblige somebody, through running his educational system or through economic interest, to speak your language, to some extent you are imposing your pattern of thought on him. A contemporary French writer puts it like this: 'Only knowledge of language enables the influence of the culture expressed by that language to be fully effective and to reach the soul of another people.' This is certainly true. A Tunisian once said to me, of French influence, 'They have civilised me to the depths of my soul.' He said it with great bitterness. When at conferences of UNESCO (the United Nations Educational, Scientific and Cultural Organization) French-speaking Africans and English-speaking Africans get up to address the assembly, you can at once recognise in them representatives of British and French culture: the French-speaking Africans, speaking in a rather eloquent, logical way, the British more blunt, empirical, occasionally even humorous. In this international organisation,

UNESCO, which was set up in 1946 to promote cultural exchanges on a basis of equality between all its members, the four languages in which all official transactions take place are four European languages. English, French, Spanish and Russian. It has had five Director-Generals since it was initiated, an Englishman, an American, an Italian, a Mexican (I don't know how he got in!) and a Frenchman – the Frenchman is now Director-General. It has in fact become an agency for propagating European culture. It has a budget, 80% of which is provided by the United States, the Soviet Union, Japan and 11 Western European countries. It concentrates over 75% of its expenditure on education, science and technology, as conceived of in the advanced countries of the northern hemisphere. World-wide, UNESCO estimates that about 700 million people are illiterate and it aims to use a massive programme of television and radio to remedy this deficiency. There will of course, be programmes in indigenous languages, but the dominant European languages will also be used to a very large extent. In the process the ex-illiterates will be made more susceptible to mass propaganda and mob emotion, and via Telstar and its marvels they will in due course be able to watch the heavyweight boxing championship and even perhaps graduate to 'Dad's Army' and 'Up Pompeii'!

I don't want to suggest that this is something that is being imposed upon them. The process of auto-indoctrination has long ago set in. There are many Africans and Asians who do not regard themselves as the victims of cultural exploitation; they absorb and imitate everything very eagerly just as, for example, the Japanese have done. Above all, they have absorbed what, for want of a better word, I would call the anthropocentric idea of man as the centre of the universe. I quote from a speech made in 1966 by the Deputy Director-General of UNESCO Malcolm Adiseshia, who is in fact an Indian: 'We must plan and execute a more dynamic programme of education, of critical study and reflection and of scientific research, based clearly and explicitly on the doctrine that man is the *summum bonum* of existence.'

I want in the closing minutes to examine what this anthropocentric doctrine is, where it seems to have led and to be leading. What is its scale of values? It developed after the gradual rejection, beginning in the 18th century, of the Christian idea of original sin: for the idea that every man comes into the world with some kind of debt and obligation, it has substituted the idea that everyone comes into the world with certain inalienable rights. This has been expressed perhaps most clearly in the American Declaration of Independence: 'All men are endowed by their creator with certain inalienable rights ... life, liberty and the pursuit of happiness.' Since the Creator has conferred these rights and He is omnipotent, if we feel deprived of them then it is His fault. We are aggrieved; we are suffering injustice. We resent, therefore, being ill or poor, or growing old or indeed dying. This conclusion is already sufficiently absurd in itself, but unfortunately, as men have ceased to believe in a creator, they have more and more come to believe in the power of the state. Thus today, if our pursuit of happiness is frustrated, we are inclined to blame the government – from this in part derives the philosophy of the welfare state and the assumption that happiness is in some way connected with good hygiene, an unlimited supply of consumer goods and paid holidays on the Costa Brava. Edward T. Hall, the American anthropologist, who has made a special study of culture as communication between different peoples, seems in some curious way to assume that happiness is an almost tangible commodity of which the United States has the monopoly. He relates in his book how Professor Daniel Lerner, 'a sociologist at the Massachusetts Institute of Technology, discovered when he interviewed villagers in Turkey that the idea of achieving happiness did not mean anything to them. It had never entered their minds that happiness was one of the things that you had a right to expect from life and might strive to achieve.' It does not seem to have entered Professor Lerner's head that he and the villagers might have been better off without this idea of happiness, or indeed without the worship of youth, wealth and power and the fear of poverty, old age and death.

Secondly, one feature of this concept of culture and civilisation, which we have imported into the less favoured countries, is the atomisation of society, the breakdown of the original organic forms of society. This follows directly from what I've just been saying, since happiness, however we define it, is clearly a subjective state; in other words it can only be determined in relation to an individual. Therefore our society has tended to become broken up into its smallest components, that is, individual egotists seeking their happiness. When these individuals in the mass feel their happiness and interests threatened, they come together temporarily as mobs, but not as new units in the organisation of a new society. This atomisation of society, together with industrialisation, which of course has very much contributed to the process of disintegration, has been imported into societies which were very differently organised and therefore in Western eyes were more primitive. This disintegrative force has tended to break up societies based on the tribe and the family without having anything much to put in their place. I talked recently to a student from Uganda, who told me he had been repelled when he first came to Britain not by racialism, as such, but by what he described as the coldness of the British people, who had no community feeling and seemed fast to be losing feeling for the family as well. He said that when he and his friends, who had been educated in the west, came back home, they found themselves tempted, instead of going to live with their families, to live in an air-conditioned hotel room where they could be at peace with their books. He was genuinely torn between the feeling for his traditional way of life and community, and the individualism which he felt had been inculcated into him in the West.

Finally, we are teaching these other communities through western science and technology to destroy their environment, as we have very largely destroyed ours. It is estimated that every year one million tons of sulphuric acid fall on Sweden – not one of the most highly industrialised countries. I suppose in due course an even heavier load will fall on central Africa. Less progressive peoples in other continents used to preserve their environment and its natural resources by attributing a feeling of divinity to nature. In an article by Clare Stirling in a recent issue of the *Sunday Times*, entitled 'The Great Assuwan Folly', she says, 'Five thousand years ago the people of the Nile Valley used to throw virgins into the river every August to appease Hapi, the god of the flood. Until the coming of the dam, the Nile's annual flood remained one of nature's exquisitely balanced wonders, Egypt's principal source of life.' She went on to explain how today, because the silt cannot pass through the dam, the larger areas which it used to fertilise either are not fertilised or can only be fertilised by importing artificial fertilisers at great expense; how the balance of salinity in the eastern Mediterranean is being disturbed and how the Nile Delta is now being eroded by the rush of clean water. In this way something which was built with the best intentions, is demonstrating how man in his greed, his arrogance and his ignorance is creating a natural disaster, where primitive man might have shown more wisdom.

So at the end of this rather depressing story we are still left with the fact that, in terms of human contact and meaningful communication, East is still East, and West is still West. But in large areas, which include Western technology and Western political thinking, whether in the form of communism or capitalism, the Asian and African countries have proved only too ready pupils. The latest conquest of the northern hemisphere is the conquest of space and so we have the happy spectacle of a Chinese satellite circling the globe emitting the message 'the East is Red', whilst American astronauts practise their golf shots on the surface of the moon. And one is tempted to think that it might have been better to attempt a conquest more difficult, but perhaps equally important; the conquest of man's own nature by himself.

About Idries Shah

BORN IN 1924, into an aristocratic Afghan family, Idries Shah created a large body of literary work, most of which considered elements of "Eastern Thought", especially Sufism and Sufi thought. Some of his best known works include The Sufis and several collections of teaching stories featuring Nasrudin.

Shah devoted his life to collecting, selecting and translating Sufi books and key works of Sufi classical literature, adapting them to the needs of the West and disseminating them in the Occident.

Called by some "practical philosophy", by others "templates in straight thinking" – these works represent centuries of Sufi thought and Islamic thought aimed at the development of human potential to its fullest extent.

They stress virtues such as commonsense, clear-thinking and humor to counter cant and religious dogma. As such they are vital works in the area of Islamic philosophy, and may be viewed as an antidote to radicalism and fanaticism much needed in the world today.

Shah's books have been translated into dozens of languages, have sold in their millions, and are regarded as a cultural bridge between West and East. His work and contribution to Sufism are represented by The Idries Shah Foundation.

About ISF

ISF IS DEVOTED to championing a sense of imagination, and to teaching stories – the kind of which are contained in the large published corpus of the writer and thinker, Idries Shah.

Engaged in a wide range of charitable projects on a world-wide basis, the Foundation seeks to stimulate the minds of both young and old by regarding the world in new ways.

In collaboration with UNESCO, ISF has begun a major story-writing competition for children in five languages and 180 countries. Other projects are working to give illustrated books to kids in Afghanistan and other conflict zones on a mass scale, thereby sparking the innate sense of imagination in young minds.

Yet another endeavour is striving to build the first global StoryBank bridging disparate societies through stories – which we regard as the essence of all culture.

Thank you for your support of ISF, and your interest in our projects.

An Eye to the Future
Dr. Alexander King, Dr. Martin Holdgate, Eugene Grebenik, Dr. Kenneth Mellanby, George McRobie

East and West, Today and Yesterday
Sir Stephen Runciman, Patrick O'Donovan, Peter Brent, Sir Roger Stevens, Nirad C. Chaudhuri, Iris Butler, Prof. G.M. Carstairs, Richard Harris

Science and the Paranormal
Leonard Lewin, D.Sc.

Sufic Traces in Georgian Literature
Katharine Vivian

Rembrandt and Angels
Michael Rubinstein

Biological and Cultural Evolution
Mary Midgley

The Age of Anxiety: a Reassessment
Malcolm Lader

Goethe's Scientific Consciousnes
Henri Bortoft

The Healing Within: Medicine, Health and Wholeness
Robin Price

A Clash of Cultures: The Malaysian Experience
David Widdicombe, Q.C.

Evaluating Spiritual and Utopian Groups *Arthur J. Deikman, M.D.*

Malta's Ancient Temples and Ruts
Rowland Parker & Michael Rubinstein

The Pagan Saviours: Pagan Elements in Christian
Ritual and Doctrine
Contributed by Cultural Research Services

The Marketing of Christianity: The Evolution of
Early Christian Doctrine
Contributed by Cultural Research Services

The Press Gang: The World in Journalese
Philip Howard

Taboos: Structure and Rebellion
Lynn Holden

Paranormal Perception? A Critical Evaluation
Christopher C. French

The Unseen World: The Rise of Gods and Spirits
Contributed by Cultural Research Services

Godmakers: The First Idols
Contributed by Cultural Research Services

The Universal Ego
Alexander King

Conclusions from Controlled UFO Hoaxes
David Simpson

Jokes and Groups
Christie Davies

Creative Translation
David Pendlebury

The Crusades as Connection: Cultural transfer
during the Holy Wars
Contributed by Cultural Research Services

Baptised Sultans: The contribution of Frederick II
of Sicily in the transfer and adaptation of
Oriental ideas to the West
Contributed by Cultural Research Services

Brain Development During Adolescence and Beyond
Dr. Sarah-Jayne Blakemore

Collective Behaviour and the Physics of Society
Philip Ball

Counter-Intuition
Dr. Kevin Byron

Music, Pleasure and the Brain
Dr. Harry Witchel

Fields of the Mind
Dr. Rupert Sheldrake

Why do we leave it so late?
David Canter

Scheherazade and the global mutation of
teaching stories
Robert Irwin

Consciousness, will and responsibility
Chris Frith

Extraordinary Voyages of the Panchatantra
Ramsay Wood

www.ingramcontent.com/pod-product-compliance
Lightning Source LLC
Chambersburg PA
CBHW020609030426
42337CB00013B/1281